Mini-Wife Syndrome:
A Divorced Dad's Guide

Katie Lee Douglas

CONTENTS

INTRODUCTION

Uh…hello…

My name is Katie.

This is the first time I've ever written a book specifically for men, so this is… um… a bit awkward for me.

Chances are it's a bit awkward for you, too, right? After all, you're only reading this book because your wife or girlfriend handed it to you.

She looked pretty desperate, too, didn't she?

Or maybe you are the one looking pretty desperate. Desperately trying to understand what in the heck she's talking about… this Mini-Wife thing… and you happened across this book.

Okay…. Deep breath. It's fine either way. We'll get through this.

The fact is, I am writing this book for you… to try to help you understand this thing called Mini-Wife Syndrome… because I know how hard it is for you to understand and how hard it is for your spaghetti-brained wife to explain it to your waffle-head. I know because I've tried it. I've…

What's that? You don't understand what I mean… spaghetti? Waffles?

Oh… I guess you haven't read that book, huh?

Okay, what I'm talking about is brains. You know... women have brains like spaghetti, all emotional and jumbled up, with everything affecting everything else. Men have brains like waffles... all compartmentalized. I'm told that you guys have compartments for work, compartments for wife, compartments for kids... I wouldn't know since I'm a girl, but...*

Are you getting the picture?

No?

Okay... Let me put it this way... women and men just think differently.

And why I'm saying this is to let you know that even though this thing, this Mini-Wife Syndrome, might seem trivial to you, it's NOT trivial to your wife. In fact, it's like a long piece of rotten spaghetti polluting up many areas of her life, not just the compartment devoted to "husband" or "stepdaughter."

That's why it's so important for you to understand. Because this little thing that you have compartmentalized along with the other waffle syrup in your "wife" compartment (admit it, at this point you really do believe it's all in her head, don't you?) can and will wreck your marriage!

So read on and I promise I will try to explain Mini-Wife Syndrome to you as compartmentally and as succinctly as possible.

And hopefully you and your wife will thank me in the end.

*References to waffles and spaghetti are from an analogy from Men are Like Waffles, Women are Like Spaghetti by Bill & Pam Farrel.

WHAT IN THE HECK IS A MINI-WIFE ANYWAY?

A Mini-Wife is a daughter of a divorced dad who has become his primary companion and confidante in the absence of a significant other in his life. (It is totally non-sexual in nature.)

Dads of daughters with Mini-Wife Syndrome are often characterized as "awesome dads," the ones who essentially give up their lives to make their daughters happy. The problem often goes unnoticed until Dad develops a serious relationship with a more appropriately-aged female who starts to feel that things are a little "off."

But isn't she just jealous???

Well, of course she's jealous! And with good reason.

After all, who signs up for marriage with a man for better or for worse, to have and to hold, and to be his number... uh... two???

And before you start feeling all guilty at the mere thought of putting your wife first, let me assure you Mini-Wife Syndrome is NOT good for your daughter, either.

Because in its severest forms, what we are very sweetly calling Mini-Wife Syndrome has a very different name in the world of psychology… one that doesn't sound quite so nice. It is called Emotional Incest and its harmful effects are well-documented.

Again… Emotional Incest is non-sexual in nature, but it is essentially a type of altered relationship where a child is placed in a role more suited to an adult and essentially used as emotional support for an adult. Kids in this position often do not do well in future relationships. Studies have shown that adults who were victims of Emotional Incest grow up to be passive-aggressive, narcissistic, and worse. Depending on how long and how far the Emotional Incest has been allowed to go, parents of these children might consider family counseling.

But I digress.

We are here to discuss common, everyday Mini-Wife Syndrome, what it is, what problems it causes for both your wife and your daughter, and most importantly, what you can do about it.

WHY WOULD YOU CALL MY DAUGHTER A MINI-WIFE?

Below is a very succinct run-down of the symptoms of Mini-Wife Syndrome. Try to look at them objectively. In my experience, it is very hard for a father to see fault in his daughter. Try to think of these as symptoms of a bigger problem, not faults. Not every Mini-Wife will have every symptom, but if you see your daughter in more than a couple of them, I think it's safe to say you do, indeed, have a Mini-Wife in your marriage.

Mini-Wives tend to occur more frequently, and perhaps be more pronounced in relationships where the father has been single for a long period of time. This is pretty self-explanatory. If you have been single for a long time, it has likely given your daughter time to settle into the "wife" role in your life and home.

Since Mini-Wives are accustomed to the sole attention of their fathers, if there comes a time when she is NOT the center of his attention, she might punish him by pouting, whining, or ignoring him. Mini-Wife daughters seem to struggle with entertaining themselves. If they aren't receiving the bulk of your attention, they might pout, become angry, or misbehave in order to draw attention to themselves. For the Mini-Wife, negative attention from Daddy is better than no attention at all.

The Mini-Wife may be overly affectionate towards her father, and might even be inappropriate in her affections. This is one of the harder symptoms for a father to recognize, simply because he doesn't know what is appropriate and what is not, and this differs from family to family. Suffice it to say, in a "normal" father-daughter relationship, physical affection declines as the child grows older and should be gently curtailed by the time the child begins developing breasts.

The Mini-Wife may become angry or hurt with her father for showing physical affection to her stepmother. Your daughter might push herself between you and your wife when you are hugging or kissing, she might click her tongue or sigh loudly, or just tell you outright she doesn't like it. You might have problems walking in public next to your wife because your daughter is constantly under your feet in an attempt to maneuver herself between the two of you. She may even take your hand and try to pull you away from her stepmother.

The Mini-Wife might seem obsessed with her father. For instance, she might call you several times a day or insist on speaking with you on the phone while you're out with your wife. She might be overly interested in every aspect of your life rather than developing a life of her own.

The Mini-Wife insists on private dates with Dad. She doesn't want to share you with another woman, and while this might seem reasonable and even cute, it is a trait more suited to a wife than a daughter.

The Mini-Wife feels she has equal standing with her stepmother. She might tattle to you about her stepmother, feel she has the right to be included in decisions that are more suited to adults, or feel she has as much or more influence over you than does her stepmother. If you feel you need to "keep the peace" in your home, more like a polygamist marriage than two married people with a child, then you probably have a Mini-Wife in your marriage.

The Mini-Wife cherishes past memories or the time before stepmother was in the picture. And she brings them up liberally. The purpose of this is to have an exclusive moment with Daddy that cannot possibly include the stepmother who cannot participate in the memory. It also serves to remind the stepmother that she came AFTER the Mini-Wife and in the spaghetti-minds of women, that somehow that gives the stepmother less stature in the triangle.

The Mini-Wife speaks in a "babyish" voice and engages in "helpless" or "Damsel in Distress" behavior. If your daughter seems "accident prone" and constantly in need of comfort for all her little bumps and bruises, you might have a Mini-Wife. If she is forever being "bullied" and in need of protection, you might have a Mini-Wife. If she is nearly as tall as you but still needs you to cut up her pancakes, you most probably have a Mini-Wife. Daughters of divorced dads constantly look for ways to command his attention. These are some of the oldest female tricks in the book and girls are born knowing how to use them.

The Mini-Wife feels like she is the Woman of the House. Or at least as much the Woman of the House as her stepmother. If your daughter becomes offended because her stepmother changed something about the house or the way it is run, you might have a Mini-Wife.

Mini-Wives try to "take care" of Daddy. If your daughter wants to make your plate, fill your glass, do your laundry, or excessively looks for ways to help you, she probably is trying to be your helpmate. It is a wife's job to be your primary helpmate and has been since Eve was created as a helpmeet to Adam. It might seem cute and harmless to you, but to your wife it is just another way the Mini-Wife manages to steal her rightful place in the home and marriage.

Mini-Wives jump at any chance to side with Daddy against their stepmother. Even if you are simply joking around with your wife, anything that can possibly be perceived as a divide between the two of you will find Mini-Wife jumping on Daddy's bandwagon to team up against and exclude her stepmother.

HOW IN THE WORLD
DID THIS HAPPEN?

Let me say right off the bat, I am not a psychologist. Though I have taken (and Aced, I might add) the couple of Psychology courses required in college, I am more a self-study in marriage and relationships and an observer of people.

That said, I have a few theories of my own as to what might cause Mini-Wife Syndrome and what might be done to help these girls overcome it and perhaps begin to develop in a healthier way. Just remember, these are the theories of a NON-professional. If you notice developmental or psychological problems in your child, please take them to see a qualified therapist.

Electra Complex

When my daughter was three years old, she became seriously attached to her biological father, to whom I was still married at the time. Even though she had always been a "Mama's girl" to that point, this new behavior didn't concern me because I recognized it as perfectly natural female development.

It is normal, and even desirable, for little girls to become strongly attracted to their fathers during their preschool years. Their father is and should be their "first love." Some little girls might even verbalize they wish to marry their father when they grow up. This stage of development is very important for little girls to experience because they are learning gender development. Sigmund Freud called this stage *Reverse Oedipus Complex* but later psychologists have termed it the *Electra Complex*.

During this time, the little girl might try very hard to replace her mother in her father's affections, but as the marriage progresses unaffected, she gradually arrives at the conclusion that she is unable to compete with the much older, wiser woman in her father's life. At this point, a healthy little girl will give up the competition with her mother and, instead, identify with her and try to emulate her so that one day the little girl can grow up and win the love and affection of her very own prince.

In certain cases of Mini-Wife Syndrome, I believe the little girl never learns she cannot compete with her mother for her father's highest affections. Perhaps her parents divorced too early for this process to occur or the marriage was too rocky for her to see the affection and devotion between her parents? Or perhaps she even had a stepmother present in her life but still never learned the needed lesson because she was permitted to successfully compete with her stepmother due to Dad's guilty conscience and his consequent inability to set needed boundaries. For whatever reason, she never fully came to the conclusion she could not be "the woman" in her father's life.

One of the main things a father can do to help his daughter overcome Mini-Wife Syndrome is to gently and firmly teach her that she cannot be the number one woman in his life. The sooner she recognizes this and completes this developmental task, the sooner she can begin growing into a healthy adult with healthy relationships of her own.

Guilty Dad Syndrome

Guilt is just a normal part of parenting, but the normal guilt of a parent seems to be multiplied a thousand times in fathers who have failed in their marriages. Because they were unable to make their relationships work, they tend to feel an obligation to "make it up" to their children in any possible way they can. Whereas a father still married to her mother would have no problem recognizing what is appropriate in his daughter and what is not, the guilt that fathers seem to harbor after a divorce can be a major factor in keeping a dad from teaching his daughter proper boundaries.

Whereas a non-divorced father might begin discouraging his seven year old daughter from sitting on his lap, a divorced dad might still be allowing his daughter to sit on his lap at age sixteen. And even though a man in an intact marriage might insist his child learn to sleep in her own bed by the age of three or four, a divorced dad might find himself still sharing

MINI-WIFE SYNDROME: A STEPMOTHER'S GUIDE

a bed with his twelve year old daughter.

In learning to control Mini-Wife Syndrome, a father might need to examine himself and his parenting style and if he has been parenting from guilt rather than good common sense, realize this is not an effective way to bring up a child.

Human Nature Abhors a Vacuum

As I mentioned before, many of these Mini-Wives are formed when their fathers are divorced for long periods of time. As we were all taught in elementary school that "Nature Abhors a Vacuum," so does human nature abhor a vacuum. Since the position of wife appears to be open beside a divorced man, it can easily suck a young female right on in.

The seat beside Dad is empty so his daughter fills it. She is his dinner date. She accompanies him to the movies, to the fair, even to his hair appointment. She assists him when he fixes stuff around the house. She helps him choose the curtains, their brand of toothpaste, what they will have for dinner. He is lonely so he talks to her. She is the sole recipient of all his attention and affection. She is scared at night and there is room in his double bed for her to sleep with him. Even though this is a completely non-sexual relationship, for all other intents and purposes, she is his partner in life. In effect, she is his Mini-Wife, and she rarely takes it well when another woman comes along.

It is not fair for a man to marry a woman, effectively promising her that she will be his soulmate, his best friend, and the queen of his castle, if this position is already filled. If you suspect there is a

Mini-Wife in your home and marriage, it is your obligation to correct the situation.

Emotional Incest

As I mentioned earlier, in the world of psychology, some cases of Mini-Wife Syndrome are more accurately called Emotional Incest. In its simpler form, Emotional Incest occurs when an adult uses a child to fill a void in his or her life that should be reserved for another adult. Most of the time, the divorced father has no idea he is even doing this, let alone that it can be harmful to his daughter.

Yet from Passive-Aggressive behavior to extreme Narcissism, the harmful effects of Emotional Incest are well-documented, the severity depending very much on the level the child has been allowed to immerse herself into the "adult" role.

Sometimes the mere term "Emotional Incest" grabs a father's attention when his new wife or significant other is trying to talk to him about Mini-Wife Syndrome. Most men are not even aware that Emotional Incest exists. They feel they are simply being a good father by putting so much of themselves into the relationship. However, a child is not equipped emotionally to handle adult problems and/or be an emotional support for an adult. Even though the Mini-Wife might appear to be handling the relationship well, even enjoying it, it can cause her problems with normal personality development, as well as current and future relationships. Again, if you suspect Emotional Incest has been an issue, seek family counseling.

SO…WHAT IS THE PROBLEM WITH MINI-WIFE SYNDROME?

Like any disease, Mini-Wife Syndrome comes with its own unique set of complications, not only for the Mini-Wife herself, but for the husband, the wife, and their marriage.

Mini-Wives become acutely unhappy when their father becomes interested in another woman. Since much of their self-esteem and feelings of being "special" are tied up in being their father's Mini-Wife, they tend to resent their new stepmother and feel their father no longer loves them

Fathers of Mini-Wives have problems in relationships with women. Due to the enormous commitment a father has to his Mini-Wife, he can't seem to put his whole self into building a new relationship with a woman he might desire as wife. If he does manage to remarry, then his new wife might feel she is living with the "other woman." It is often a struggle for a stepmother to love another woman's child, but when that child is her biggest competition for the love, attention, and approval of her husband, it is next to impossible. Life can become hellacious for the man caught in the middle of a power struggle between his wife and daughter. There is little chance for peace in his home until a hierarchy is established, and this is often difficult for the father of a Mini-Wife.

Stepmothers feel there's "something missing" in their relationships with their husbands. And they are right. If a husband already has a "best friend," a "life confidant," or basically a "life partner," they have no business getting married. No wonder second marriages have up to a 75% chance of ending in divorce where stepchildren are concerned.

Mini-Wives grow up to have problems with their own relationships. After all, where is she to find someone who will treat her as well as her father? Fathers are mature, grown men with an instinct toward protecting and caring for their daughters. When they are cast in the wrong role in their daughter's minds, it stands to reason that no man her age can compete.

Stepmothers lose respect for husbands who allow Mini-Wife Syndrome to continue. And you thought we were only jealous, didn't you? The hard fact is, Guys, that what we feel goes well beyond jealousy. We see you bamboozled, manipulated, and basically led around by the nose by a little girl and we feel... disgust. How can we possibly respect you as a man when you can't/won't control one little girl? If you want the respect of your wife, Guys, then you've got to open your eyes and do the hard work it takes to get your daughter on a healthier, more appropriate path for her life.

WHAT CAN I DO TO FIX THIS?

Now that you recognize there is a problem, I'm told that men will want to jump right on into fixing it. So let's stop beating the issue to death with what it is and what problems it can cause and get right into the meat of the matter... how to solve the problem.

I hate to tell you this, Guys, but this is not something that going to go away quickly or easily. It is probably something you're going to be dealing with for a very long time. That's why it's important for you to understand that the changes you make have to be consistent and permanent... or else Mini-Wife Syndrome will come back with a vengeance.

So the first thing you have to do is make a choice.

What??? You're asking me to choose between my wife and my daughter???

Nooooo! That's not what I'm asking. I'm asking you to look at the big picture, take some time to ponder what the future might look like, and choose between two scenarios.

Here. I'll help you out...

Scenario #1: *Ignore the problem/let the status quo reign.*

Your wife and your daughter continue to argue and fight like cats and dogs.

You inevitably get stuck in the middle. You try to keep the peace, be fair, mediate, referee...

Your daughter thinks you are taking your wife's side. She pouts, cries, throws tantrums, ups her game and competes with your wife even more.

Your wife thinks you are taking your daughter's side. She whines, cries, fusses, nags, gives ultimatums...

Finally, you and your wife divorce.

My condolences. You are one of the 75% of couples in second marriages who didn't make it because of the stepkids.

Your daughter is ecstatic. She no longer has to compete with your wife. She is again the woman of the household, but this time she will be on the lookout and even more adamantly opposed to any other woman in your home.

The years go by. You are in and out of relationships but none lasts for too long (for reasons we've already discussed). You have your daughter, so you are not too bothered by this.

Your daughter is in and out of relationships, but she seems to be having issues, as well. By now she might have been in a couple of troubled marriages of her own. You are now taking care of her and one or more of her offspring.

Maybe you'll live like this until you die. Grow old with your Mini-Wife. Don't be surprised if you feel that something is missing. Something is missing. A man is not meant to make a life and grow old with his daughter. He is meant to grow old with a wife. But you gave that up because you refused to correct the Mini-Wife behavior in your daughter when you had the chance. So you grow old and die.

But what happens to your daughter?

She has relationship problems. She doesn't know how to relate to men her age. Maybe she'll find someone older than her who reminds her of you. Maybe she'll marry him. Maybe this will happen before you die. But then you'd be left alone without someone to grow old with.

Regrets are many.

Horrible scenarios, aren't they? One could go on with these morbid thoughts all day long.

Don't you wish you'd done the hard work and corrected Mini-Wife Syndrome? Aren't you glad I'm here to help you with that? I'm certain you are.

Scenario #2: *You work with your wife to correct Mini-Wife Syndrome in your daughter.*

Your wife is happier, more hopeful, perhaps a bit impatient…

Your daughter is upset, miserable, angry, thinks you don't love her…

You spend time reassuring both your wife and your daughter you love them. You just do it in appropriate ways so that everyone is moving toward the goals you have set.

You work to strengthen your marriage with your wife.

You work to strengthen independence with your daughter.

You no longer get caught in the middle because proper boundaries have been set with both your wife and your daughter.

There is peace in your home.

You stay married!

Congratulations! You are one of the 25% of second marriages who make it despite the stepkids.

Your daughter marries a wonderful man who treats her as well as you treat your wife. She brings the grandkids over to visit at least once a week.

You grow old together with your wife.

Regrets are few.

Sooo… as I was saying…

The first thing you have to do is choose between the two scenarios, and IF you choose to work on the problem, IF you choose to make a hard and fast commitment to keeping your marriage and raising your daughter in a healthy way, the next step is to be consistent. Super consistent. *Brutally* consistent.

But in order to be consistent, you first have to take care of any *Guilty Dad Syndrome* you might have lurking around in your psyche.

I, for one, am convinced that many of the problems that come from kids having divorced parents are a result of guilty parenting. Many kids of divorce become entitled, materialistic, narcissistic, and spoiled, all because everybody makes them into little victims and they carry this victimhood with them into adulthood.

In order for anyone to be an effective parent, they have to parent from good common sense, *not guilt!* Parenting decisions should not be made "off the cuff" or based on "gut feelings." Why? Because feelings aren't valid. Results are valid. Doing what is right is valid.

So make it a priority to think about what you are doing as a parent and what the results will be before you make any major parenting decisions. Resolve in your head that you are doing what you are doing for the ultimate good of your daughter and put away any guilty feelings you have for correcting Mini-Wife Syndrome.

Remember, feelings aren't always valid. Results & outcome are valid.

WORKING WITH YOUR WIFE TO CORRECT MINI-WIFE SYNDROME

Okay... you've made the decision to correct Mini-Wife Syndrome and you've put away any guilty feelings you might have about your decision. Now you need to involve your wife in helping you correct the problem.

I know, I know... it feels wrong and unfair to involve your wife, kinda like you're ganging up on your daughter or something, right? Because up until this point you have looked yourself as being the referee between your wife and your daughter but you *have not taken sides*.

You've got to start changing your mindset.

Start to see your wife as your team member. You are supposed to be a united team with your wife, remember? You are NOT on a team with your daughter. You were never meant to be on a team with your daughter. That is not in her Job Description. So choose your wife's side!

Furthermore, if you do not involve your wife, she is going to be frustrated and feel like you're not doing anything to correct the problem. She is going to want to see results right away and not understand that even though you are working on the problem, it is going to take some time to get things under control.

If she is involved in the decision making process from the beginning, she will be in more of a position to be patient and understanding while you work with your daughter in the gentlest manner possible.

Plus you need her input. You need her spaghetti brain to understand the problems and even see that they exist.

Begin a dialogue with your wife. Ask for her help. Trust the woman you married. She might not seem very loving toward your daughter at this season in your lives, but trust me, if she loves you she will have a hard time doing harm to your flesh and blood. Trust her good heart to help you help your daughter. Also make it clear you are doing this for *her*, because you have chosen to grow old with her.

With your wife's help, make a list of all the symptoms of Mini-Wife Syndrome that your daughter is exhibiting. These do not necessarily have to be limited to the symptoms I have listed in this book. This is *your* family, *your* unique set of problems, and *your* plan. Once you've identified the problems, brainstorm with your wife as to what can be done to manage the symptoms with the two goals in mind: putting your wife in her place as the #1 woman in your life and supporting your daughter through the changes as gently as possible.

For example, a plan for my household that includes myself (Katie Lee), my husband (Big D) and my stepdaughter (Shell) might read as follows:

Problem #1: Shell is overly affectionate with her father, even to the point of being inappropriate.

Goal: Big D will gradually withdraw from

excessive physical affection with Shell.

Interventions:

1. Big D will withdraw from hugs after one second

2. Big D will no longer kiss Shell on the lips. He will explain to her that it is no longer appropriate since she is growing into a young lady.

3. Big D will limit hugs/kisses with his daughter to just before leaving for work in the morning and just before going to bed at night, unless there is another legitimate reason for physical affection.

Problem #2: Shell becomes upset when Big D shows physical affection to Katie Lee.

Goal: Shell will learn to accept physical affection between Big D and Katie Lee and recognize that it is part of a healthy marriage.

Interventions:

1. Big D will explain to Shell that Katie Lee is his wife and husbands and wives are supposed to show physical affection to one another.

2. Big D will not limit physical affection to Katie Lee in the presence of his daughter.

3. Big D will provide at least double the amount of physical affection for Katie Lee than he does for his daughter.

Problem #3: Shell begs to go on private dates with Big D

Goal: Remove the potential for competition over Big D's time.

Interventions:

1. Big D will not go on private dates with Shell.

2. Big D will explain to Shell that private dates in

our families are only for couples, in our case, Big D. and Katie Lee. All other dates will be family dates including Big D., Katie Lee, Katie Lee's daughter, and Shell.

Problem #4: Shell pouts and becomes angry if she is not the center of attention.
Goal: Do not reward bad behavior with attention.
Interventions:
1. Big D will pretend not to notice if Shell is pouting.
2. Big D will discipline Shell for angry outbursts by putting her in timeout away from the family. He will do this with the least discussion possible (i.e. negative attention).
3. Big D and Katie Lee will reward Shell with positive attention for good behavior.

Problem #5: Shell tries to "team up" with Big D against Katie Lee whenever possible.
Goal: Big D and Katie Lee will remain a solid united front.
Interventions:
1. Big D will speak privately with Katie Lee of any concerns he has involving Katie Lee.
2. If Big D inadvertently opens the door for Shell to jump onto his team against Katie Lee, he will immediately make it clear he and Katie Lee are a united front.
3. Big D will never, even in play, pick on Katie Lee in the presence of Shell.

Also, keep in mind you don't have to work on every aspect of the plan all at once. You might pick two or three of the most bothersome symptoms of Mini-Wife Syndrome and begin working on them first, then gradually move on to the others. You can be gentle as long as you're firm and making progress.

DEALING WITH MINI-WIFE SYNDROME WITH YOUR DAUGHTER

The biggest, most important (and probably the hardest thing) in dealing with Mini-Wife Syndrome in your daughter is *consistency*.

You've got to be consistent in implementing the plan you've made with your wife, both in and out of her presence. Unless you seriously want to mess with your daughter's psychological development, not to mention create major trust issues in your marriage, you *cannot* revert back to being Daddy-Husband every time your wife's back is turned.

When you are alone with your daughter, it is up to YOU to protect your wife's position as Queen of the Home. In case you are unclear on what it means to be Queen of the Home, I have developed the following Chain of Command, as well as Job Descriptions for both Office of Wife and Office of Daughter.

Chain of Command

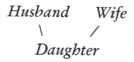

Husband   *Wife*
\   /
Daughter

Please note this does NOT read:
Husband
/   \
Wife   Daughter

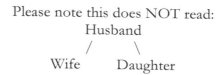

This means that your daughter should NOT feel comfortable "tattling" to you about your wife or going over your wife's head to try to persuade you to change a decision your wife has made.

Okay, now for the Job Descriptions:

Office of Wife

Primary companion of husband
Sexual companion of husband
Provides physical affection for husband
Primary helpmate of husband
Husband's Confidant
Assists with important decisions
Assists with raising children
Physically cares for husband & children

Primarily responsible for household/meals
Assists with household finances

Office of Daughter

Obeys father and stepmother
Gets an education for the future
Assists with household tasks as directed by
father and/or stepmother
Provides pleasant companionship for the
family

Are you seeing the difference?

Your wife's job is to be your best friend, to build a life and a future with you, and to grow old with you.

Your daughter's job is to learn from you, take advantage of the time she has in your household to build a future for herself, and to leave your home to grow old with someone else.

Any other arrangement is *unhealthy* and *counterproductive* to every life involved in the Mini-Wife triangle.

Guys… I cannot stress this enough. **Mini-Wife Syndrome is a disease!** It can and will kill your marriage and absolutely cripple your daughter's chance at a healthy relationship.

Start now to get this thing under control. Your peace and happiness and the future happiness of your family depends on it.

DON'T MISS IT!!!

The companion guide to
Mini-Wife Syndrome: A Divorced Dad's Guide
is now available in online bookstores!!!

Mini-Wife Syndrome:
A Stepmother's Guide

Printed in Great Britain
by Amazon